THE VICTIM'S GUIDE TO ...

Middle Age

You'll have to tell one what its like !

Jane

EXLEY

MT. KISCO, NEW YORK • WATFORD, UK

PERHAPS BIRTHDAYS ARE NOT ALWAYS THE JOYFUL OCCASIONS
THEY ONCE WERE...

... AND PERHAPS WE HAVE NOT ACHIEVED ALL OF OUR YOUTHFUL AMBITIONS ....

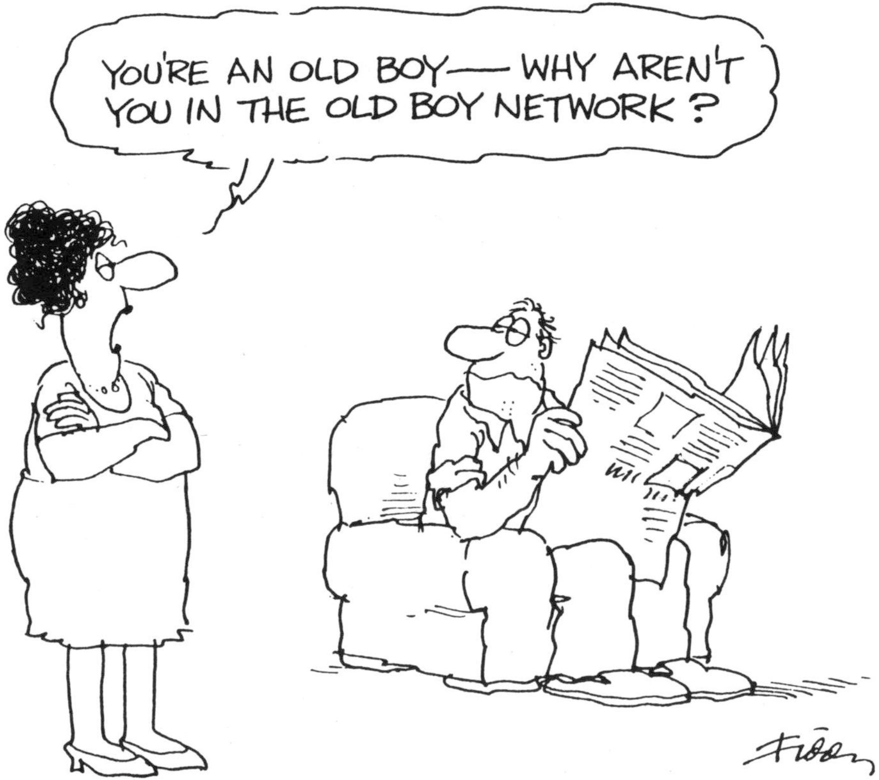
YOU'RE AN OLD BOY— WHY AREN'T YOU IN THE OLD BOY NETWORK?

... BUT THE SHOW MUST GO ON!

OF COURSE, SOME OF US AGE QUICKER THAN OTHERS...

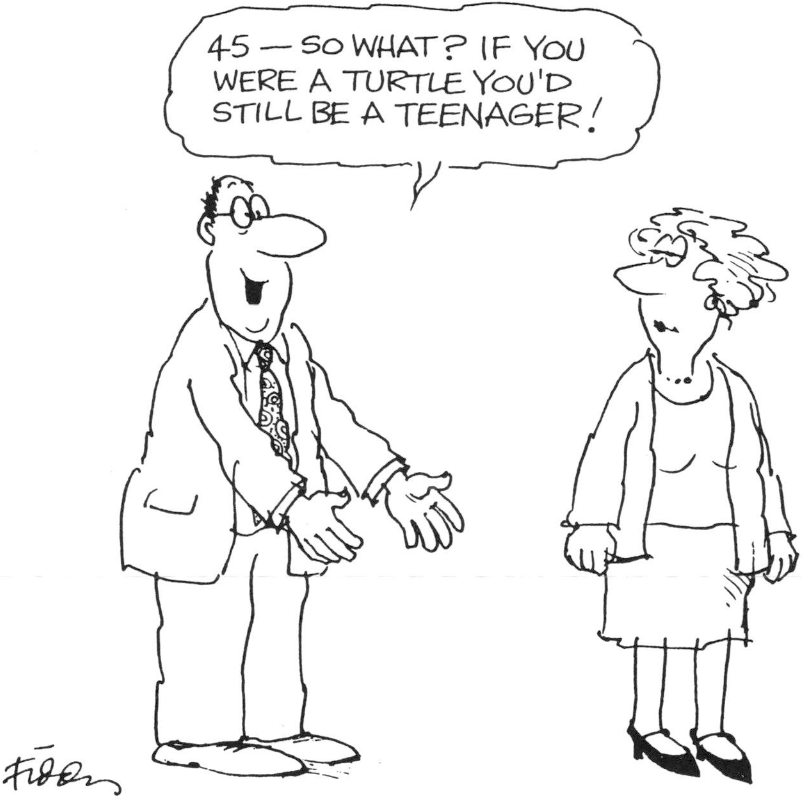
45 — SO WHAT? IF YOU WERE A TURTLE YOU'D STILL BE A TEENAGER!

DISTRIBUTION PROBLEM .

SOMETIMES THE TEMPTATION TO STOP FIGHTING
THE ADVANCING YEARS....

... IS OVERWHELMING!.....

ONE LONGS TO SWEEP IT ALL AWAY....

THE IMPORTANCE OF PHYSICAL FITNESS.
With regular exercise you can be as fit as you ever were.....

....if you ever were.

You can also enjoy the friendly greetings of fellow joggers....

... and others .

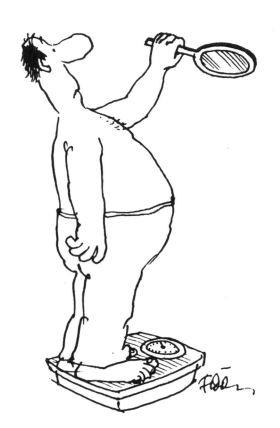

1.

2.

3.

4.

IN MIDDLE AGE IT IS IMPORTANT.....

5.

X

6.

7.

8.

... TO KEEP THE SPIRIT OF ROMANCE ALIVE ...

9.

10.

11.

12.

Roland Fiddy

.... AS LONG AS POSSIBLE.

SELF
PROTECTION
CLASSES

BUS
STOP

1.

2.

3.

4.

YOUR SEX DRIVE CAN BE AS   STRONG AS EVER....

5.

6.

....BUT SOMETIMES....

7.

8.

'PUNCH'

... IT TAKES SOME VERY ODD TURNS.

There are certain things
which are guaranteed to
make you feel middle aged....

① BOREDOM

② TWINGES

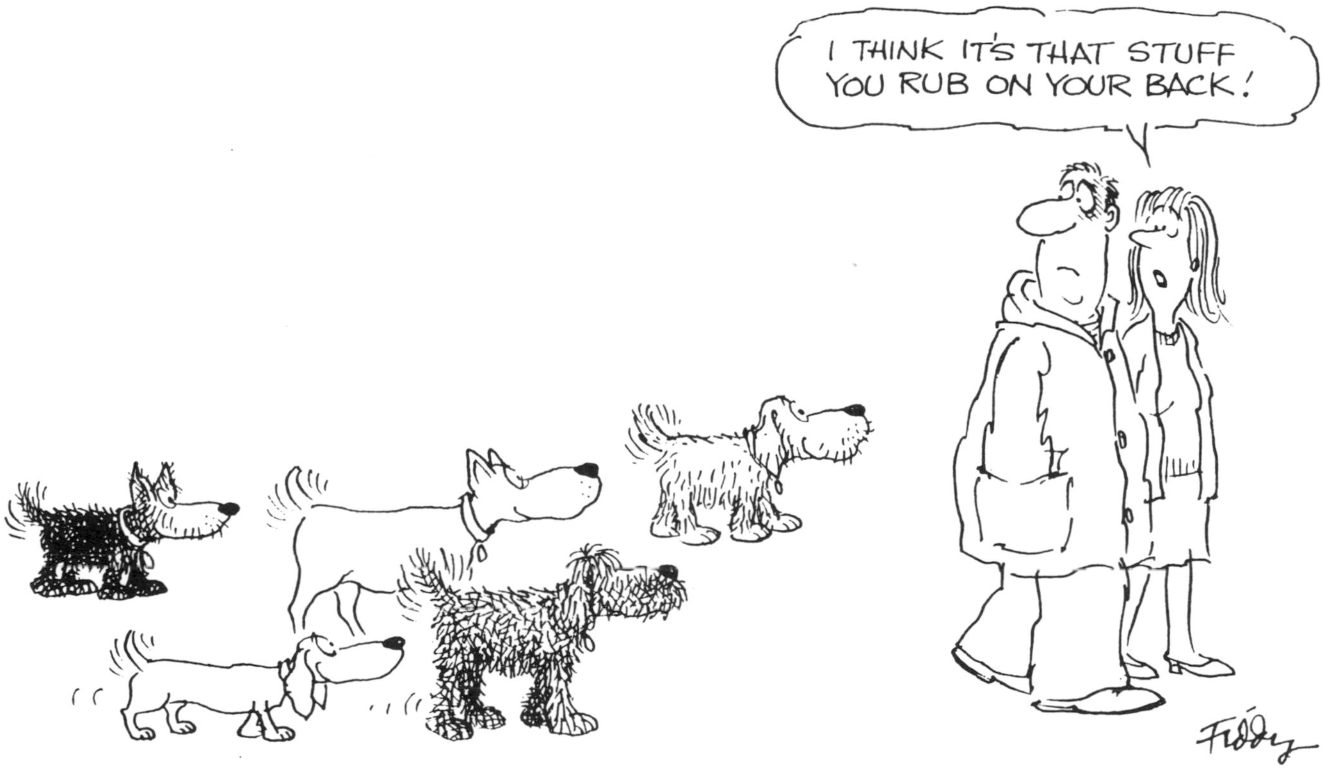
I THINK IT'S THAT STUFF YOU RUB ON YOUR BACK!

③ CHILDREN.

Twenty Good Things about being Middle Aged.

1. _ _ _ _ _ _ _ _ _ _ _
2. _ _ _ _ _ _ _ _ _ _ _
3. _ _ _ _ _ _ _ _ _ _
4. _ _ _ _ _ _ _ _ _ _ _
5. _ _ _ _ _ _ _ _ _ _ _
6. _ _ _ _ _ _ _ _ _ _
7. _ _ _ _ _ _ _ _ _ _ _ _
8. _ _ _ _ _ _ _ _ _ _ _
9. _ _ _ _ _ _ _ _ _ _
10. _ _ _ _ _ _ _ _ _ _ _

11. _ _ _ _ _ _ _ _ _ _ _ _
12. _ _ _ _ _ _ _ _ _ _ _
13. _ _ _ _ _ _ _ _ _ _ _
14. _ _ _ _ _ _ _ _ _ _ _
15. _ _ _ _ _ _ _ _ _ _ _
16. _ _ _ _ _ _ _ _ _ _ _
17. _ _ _ _ _ _ _ _ _ _ _
18. _ _ _ _ _ _ _ _ _ _ _
19. _ _ _ _ _ _ _ _ _ _ _
20. _ _ _ _ _ _ _ _ _

No, but seriously ......

There are plenty of good things about Middle Age ....

.... You're not so concerned with your "image", for one thing...

.... AND GRANDCHILDREN CAN BE A GREAT PLEASURE.

②

THE FUNNY THING ABOUT MIDDLE AGE IS....

③

.... YOU NEVER REACH IT UNTIL YOU'RE PAST IT

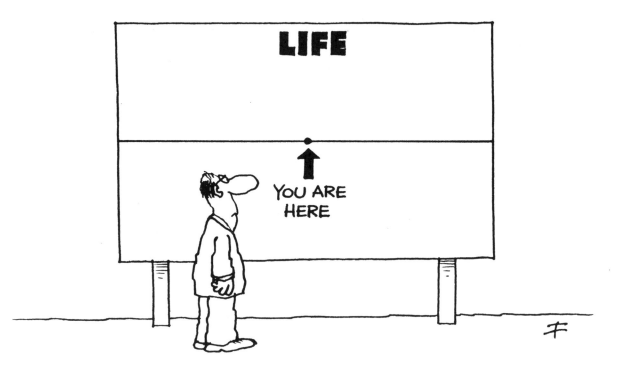

Books in the "Victim's Guide" series
($4.99 £2.99 paperback)

Award winning cartoonist Roland Fiddy sees the funny side to life's phobias, nightmares and catastrophes.

The Victim's Guide to the Dentist
The Victim's Guide to the Doctor
The Victim's Guide to Middle Age
The Victim's Guide to Air Travel

Books in the "Fanatics" series
($4.99 £2.99 paperback)

The **Fanatic's Guides** are perfect presents for everyone with a hobby that has got out of hand. Eighty pages of hilarious black and white cartoons by Roland Fiddy.

The Fanatic's Guide to the Bed
The Fanatic's Guide to Cats
The Fanatic's Guide to Computers
The Fanatic's Guide to Dads
The Fanatic's Guide to Diets
The Fanatic's Guide to Dogs
The Fanatic's Guide to Golf
The Fanatic's Guide to Husbands
The Fanatic's Guide to Money
The Fanatic's Guide to Sex
The Fanatic's Guide to Skiing

Books in the "Crazy World" series
($4.99 £2.99 paperback)

The Crazy World of Aerobics (Bill Stott)
The Crazy World of Cats (Bill Stott)
The Crazy World of Cricket (Bill Stott)
The Crazy World of Gardening (Bill Stott)
The Crazy World of Golf (Mike Scott)
The Crazy World of the Greens (Barry Knowles)
The Crazy World of The Handyman (Roland Fiddy)
The Crazy World of Hospitals (Bill Stott)
The Crazy World of Housework (Bill Stott)
The Crazy World of Learning to Drive (Bill Stott)
The Crazy World of Love (Roland Fiddy)
The Crazy World of Marriage (Bill Stott)
The Crazy World of The Office (Bill Stott)
The Crazy World of Photography (Bill Stott)
The Crazy World of Rugby (Bill Stott)
The Crazy World of Sailing (Peter Rigby)
The Crazy World of Sex (David Pye)

Books in the "Mini Joke Book" series
($6.99 £3.99 hardback)

These attractive 64 page mini joke books are illustrated throughout by Bill Stott.

A Binge of Diet Jokes
A Bouquet of Wedding Jokes
A Feast of After Dinner Jokes
A Knockout of Sports Jokes
A Portfolio of Business Jokes
A Round of Golf Jokes
A Romp of Naughty Jokes
A Spread of Over-40s Jokes
A Tankful of Motoring Jokes

Great Britain: Order these super books from your local bookseller or From Exley Publications Ltd, 16 Chalk Hill, Watford, Herts WD1 4BN. (Please send £1.30 to cover post and packaging on 1 book, £2.60 on 2 or more books.)